C000139051

TYPE 4 LOCOMOTIVES OF BRITISH RAIL

Andrew Walker and John Walker

AMBERLEY

Acknowledgements

The authors and publisher would like to thank Vaughan Hellam for permission to use copyright material in this book. All other photographs are by the authors.

First published 2018

Amberley Publishing
The Hill, Stroud
Gloucestershire, GL5 4EP

www.amberley-books.com

Copyright © Andrew Walker and John Walker, 2018

The right of Andrew Walker and John Walker
to be identified as the Author of this work has
been asserted in accordance with the Copyrights,
Designs and Patents Act 1988.

ISBN 978 1 4456 8009 5 (print)
ISBN 978 1 4456 8010 1 (ebook)

All rights reserved. No part of this book may be
reprinted or reproduced or utilised in any form
or by any electronic, mechanical or other means,
now known or hereafter invented, including
photocopying and recording, or in any information
storage or retrieval system, without the permission
in writing from the Publishers.

British Library Cataloguing in Publication Data.
A catalogue record for this book is available from
the British Library.

Origination by Amberley Publishing.
Printed in the UK.

Introduction

The six principal classes of British Rail locomotive that once made up the Type 4 classification – Classes 40, 44, 45, 46, 47 and 50 – were the survivors of a wider group that can trace its origins to the British Transport Commission's Modernisation Plan of 1955. Designating a power output of between 2,000 and 3,000 hp, the type once contained representatives of several non-standard and one-off prototype builds, including the much-loved Warship and Western diesel-hydraulics, which between them originally numbered over 100 examples.

The scrapping, exporting or accidental writing off of the numerous Type 4 prototypes in the 1960s and early 1970s – with the exception of the ten Peak Class 44s – left a cohort of diesel-electrics that became the real backbone of the BR fleet, including the most numerous single main line class ever built in Britain, the Brush 4 or Class 47 as it later became. The survival in service of several of these machines – some re-engined and designated Class 57 – over half a century after the first was built by Brush in Loughborough in 1962 is testament to their engineering quality, design fitness and versatility. It is true that the heavier and more cumbersome sixteen-wheelers of Classes 40, 44, 45 and 46 have, with the exception of a few celebrity survivors, long since gone, but for the best part of three decades they provided solid motive power for both freight and passenger operations across the entire network. The Class 50 was always a special case. Evolving from the Deltic look-a-like prototype DP2, this was arguably the outcome of a competition to enable English Electric to demonstrate that it could build a 2,700 hp machine to rival the Sulzer-powered Brush 4. An order from BR for just fifty machines hardly justified the development costs, but as with its Loughborough-built rival, a number of the 50s still earn revenue on Britain's twenty-first-century rail network.

There is no question that the Type 4s formed the indispensable core of BR's diesel fleet for many years, clocking up vast mileages on heavy freight diagrams and on many of the fastest timetabled long-distance passenger services in the country. Their disappearance from the network reflects not only the inevitability of changing technology but also the changing expectations of both freight customers and the daily travellers who take to the trains in ever increasing numbers in modern Britain. For rail enthusiasts though, they are sadly missed.

This pictorial collection features almost 200 images of BR's Type 4 diesels in photographs dating from the late 1970s to the present day and includes pictures of locomotives on freight and passenger traffic, on sheds and at works. Most of these images are, of course, unrepeatable today.

Andrew Walker
Nottingham

Type 4 Pioneer at Sheffield

The first of what might be called BR's 'production' Type 4s, the 2,000 hp English Electric Class 40, entered traffic in 1958. Class pioneer D200 (No. 40122) later became something of a celebrity and was repainted into its original green livery, following which it was much in demand for railtour duty. It is seen here at Sheffield in the summer of 1984.

Another Celebrity Machine

Like D200, No. 40106 also ended its main line BR career in green livery, but for different reasons. Having uniquely and mysteriously escaped re-painting into blue during the 1970s, its faded green colour scheme was granted a reprieve, and when No. 40106 was finally given a make-over, it emerged from the works still in its original colours. Here it passes Manchester Victoria with coke hoppers in 1982.

Heavy Duty Freight Action at Sheffield

The Type 4 locomotive fleet was deployed equally on passenger and freight duty and in this image No. 40028, formerly *Samaria*, is paired with a relative lightweight in the form of Class 25 No. 25201 as they get to grips with the Ditton–Broughton Lane oxygen tanks service at Sheffield station on a rather grim day in August 1984.

No Challenge for this 2,000 hp Machine

Despite the gradients of the Hope Valley route, this four-coach formation will be a breeze for Class 40 No. 40194, which is deputising for the more usual Class 31 on a Manchester Piccadilly to Hull service in August 1984. Here the train speeds through New Mills South Junction.

Class 40s to the Left and Right

Guide Bridge was always a hotspot for Class 40 activity, and on a typical day there would be a procession of freight and parcels services through the station. Here in September 1982 two of the class, Nos 40155 and 40168, pass on engineers' workings.

Class 40 Super Power

Not many freight diagrams demanded the power of two Class 40s, but here at Guide Bridge in September 1982 we see a Peakstone aggregates working heading for Buxton behind Nos 40177 and 40135. A pair of Class 40s was a fairly frequent sight on these services.

Double-Heading the Oxygen Tanks

Another service that regularly saw a pair of Class 40s was the Ditton–Broughton Lane BOC liquid oxygen diagram, seen here rumbling through Sheffield station with Nos 40155 and 40097 in charge in June 1982. The steep climb from Nunnery Main Line Junction up to Woodburn Junction awaits as they near their destination.

Another Pair of 40s Heads Through Sheffield

A July afternoon in 1982 sees Class 40s Nos 40022, formerly *Laconia*, and 40152 turning on the power as they head for the Hope Valley with the Broughton Lane–Ditton BOC tanks. This service ran via the Woodhead route with pairs of Class 76s until the previous July.

Superb Restoration for Original Peak

Nearly forty years old in this image, original Peak No. 44004 *Great Gable* looks resplendent in BR blue livery and with its nameplate restored to its rightful place when seen at Toton Depot's Open Weekend in August 1998.

On the Refuelling Point at Tinsley

A very overcast June morning in 1979 sees Peak Class 45 No. 45010 standing on the fuelling point at Tinsley Depot outside Sheffield. The locomotive is carrying the twin centre headcode panel configuration that would soon become obsolete as the class adopted the simpler but less attractive sealed beam headlight arrangement.

Another Split-Headcode Survivor

One of the very last Peaks to make it to the end of active life with the original split-headcode indicator configuration, No. 45027 is seen here languishing in the sidings at Swindon Works in February 1983. Introduced as D24, it had been withdrawn in 1981 after what now seems a rather brief working life.

Splendid Restoration for No. 45060

With its original split-headcode boxes restored and in working order, Peak No. 45060 *Sherwood Forester* makes a superb sight at Tinsley Depot in April 1996 on the occasion of the Open Day.

Under the Canopy at Victoria

Manchester Victoria's splendid iron platform canopy curves above Class 47 No. 47542, which has just arrived with a Liverpool service formed of Mk 1 stock on 19 January 1983.

Trans-Pennine Duty for No. 47509

Looking in very tidy external condition, Class 47 No. 47509 *Albion* waits at Huddersfield with an eastbound service on a sunny 28 September 1981. Introduced to traffic in late 1966, this was one of the class that never carried green livery.

Spacious Environs for No. 47211

Most seaside termini stations were well provided for in terms of space and platform capacity, and Scarborough was no exception to the rule. In the days before rationalisation, Class 47 No. 47211 stands at the head of a train of Mk 1 stock awaiting departure in August 1982.

Classic Unfitted Freight

Class 47 No. 47212 trundles through the site of the former Exchange station as it takes an eastbound train of open wagons towards Manchester Victoria on a bright August day in 1983. A Healey Mills-based machine at the time of this picture, No. 47212 ended its days with Freightliner, working until 2003. It was cut up at Crewe the following year.

Celebrating Channel Tunnel Freight Services

Class 47 No. 47287 stands on display at Tinsley Depot in 1996. The headboard marks the start of cross-Channel freight services from Wakefield's 'Europort' in January of that year. The green spot on the cab side denotes the multiple-working system for this sub-class. No. 47287 was withdrawn and scrapped at C. F. Booth's in nearby Rotherham in 2005.

Channel Tunnel Headboard for No. 47375

Freight services through the Channel Tunnel commenced in June 1994, and here Class 47 No. 47375 carries a commemorative headboard to mark the occasion. The smartly turned-out locomotive, named *Tinsley Traction Depot*, is seen on display at Crewe Electric Depot in October of that year. No. 47375 was exported to Hungary in 2015.

When 50s Ruled at Waterloo

Winter sunshine illuminates Class 50s Nos 50001 *Dreadnought* and 50002 *Superb* at the London terminus in February 1985. The days of locomotive-hauled services from the capital to the South and South West of England were numbered by this time.

A Visit to the Plant for No. 50033

Doncaster's famous Plant locomotive works plays hosts to Class 50 No. 50033 *Glorious* in July 1984. The entire Class 50 fleet went through the works here during the refurbishment programme of the late 1970s, and they continued to visit for repair and maintenance thereafter. No. 50020 *Revenge* is also visible.

Class 50s Await their Turn

This is Clapham Junction Carriage Sidings in September 1988, with a pair of NSE-liveried Class 50s standing with empty stock between turns. On the left is No. 50027 *Lion*, with No. 50048 *Dauntless* alongside. Both locomotives were withdrawn in 1991, and while No. 50048 was cut up in Glasgow in 1992, *Lion* survives in preservation, one of many Class 50s to escape the scrapyard.

Colourful 50s at New Street

A pair of NSE-liveried Class 50s brightens up the scene at Birmingham New Street in March 1987. At the head of a passenger service in the foreground is No. 50034 *Furious* while No. 50035 *Ark Royal* runs light engine beyond. Both locomotives were withdrawn from main line service in 1990, though No. 50034 was not to survive into preservation.

Split-Headcode Machine Awaits Cutting Up

The characterful 'split-headcode' 40s were a favourite with many enthusiasts. Here, No. 40139 stands at Crewe Works after withdrawal, with Nos 40008 and 40006 behind, in March 1984.

A Studious Note-Taker

A young spotter diligently records numbers in this 1984 study of Class 40 No. 40073 at Crewe Works. This was one of the individuals that had its white headcode discs removed at some point. Behind is No. 40131 and the duo is joined by a Class 81 electric, No. 81001, another veteran of the post-steam era.

No More Freight Duties for These Type 4s

In the industrial surroundings of the works at Crewe, numerous Class 40s await their final visit to the scrapyard. In this early 1984 view Nos 40115 and 40088 stand in the sidings while in the background are Nos 40065 and 40023.

No. 40191 at the Works

No. 40191 heads a line of condemned locomotives at Crewe in March 1984. Keeping the Class 40 company here are 25 kV electric No. 81001 and two more 40s, Nos 40131 and 40073.

Split-Headcode Machine at Guide Bridge

Sporting a somewhat bleached pair of nose-end doors, 'split-headcode' Class 40 No. 40141 takes a short mixed freight through Guide Bridge and towards Dewsnap Sidings in September 1982.

Newspaper Shunt at Guide Bridge

Class 40 No. 40013, formerly *Andania*, another victim of the headcode disc removal policy, marshals a short train of newspaper vans at Guide Bridge station. A group of spotters is camped out at the end of the platform.

Last Days of the Semaphores

Class 40 No. 40077 heads a classic unfitted mixed freight at Treeton South Junction on 2 July 1982. The multitude of semaphore signals at this location was soon to disappear as the Sheffield area modernisation plan was rolled out. No. 40077 itself had less than a year left in traffic at this point.

Every Semaphore Tells a Story

The signal on the left of this picture once controlled access to the Midland branch line from Cudworth to Barnsley. The arm has gone but the post remains as Class 40 No. 40196 powers through the site of the former station with a mixed freight in May 1982. Soon all the semaphores in this picture would be consigned to history.

A Northbound Crossover at Royston

The Midland main line at Royston Junction near Barnsley suffered badly from mining subsidence, hence the need for this northbound passenger service to cross from fast to slow lines, avoiding the worst affected trackwork. Peak No. 46046 is seen on a rake of Mk 1 stock in May 1982.

Peak at Ravensthorpe

Peak Class 45 No. 45117 speeds through Ravensthorpe station near Dewsbury with a Newcastle–Liverpool express in the summer of 1983. Even this modest station merited some superb wrought-iron canopy work courtesy of the Victorian railway builders.

HST Rake on the Move

Peak Class 45 No. 45049 *The Staffordshire Regiment (The Prince of Wales's)* is seen here at a somewhat overcast Sheffield in May 1982. With a restaurant car acting as a barrier vehicle, the Peak is taking a rake of HST stock to Derby, possibly from Neville Hill. (V. Hellam)

Atmospheric Cudworth North

Surrounded by relics of a bygone railway age, Class 45 No. 45017 heads past Cudworth North Junction with a southbound mineral working on 3 October 1984. The branch to the glassworks at Monk Bretton, built by the Midland Railway and still served by rail in 2018, can be seen diverging ahead of the train. No. 45017 later became departmental locomotive No. ADB968024. (V. Hellam)

Royal Power for the Royal Mail

Class 47 No. 47798 *Prince William* speeds through the centre roads at Stafford station with a southbound mail service. The date was April 2001. The locomotive has since been refurbished but still carries its royal insignia.

XP64 Recreation at New Street

Class 47 No. 47853 carried the experimental XP64 livery, the precursor to BR's standard blue livery, as D1733 in 1964. The colour scheme was later recreated, as seen here at Birmingham in 2002. The locomotive had recently been named *Rail Express*. No. 47853 is still in service as part of the DRS fleet.

Inverness Sleeper Waits to Leave Queen Street

Traces of blue remain in the sky as No. 47593 *Galloway Princess* stands at Glasgow's Queen Street terminus with the stock of a sleeper service to Inverness in June 1985. Additional coaches will be added to the train at Perth.

No. 47805 in the South Coast Sunshine

Sunny Eastbourne is the location of this 1996 image of InterCity-liveried Class 47 No. 47805. The Brush 4 is waiting to depart with a cross-country service comprising a short rake of Mk 2 stock while two of the classic Southern Region EMUs occupy adjacent platforms. No. 47805 survives in service as part of the DRS fleet.

Waverley Railtour Duty for No. 47823

Class 47 No. 47823 worked a 'Green Express' railtour from Sheffield to Edinburgh on 28 August 1993 and is seen here at Waverley awaiting departure on the return leg. Previously carrying the number 47163, this Brush 4 was adorned with a Union Jack to commemorate the Queen's Silver Jubilee in 1977.

A Former Western Region Machine in Yorkshire

Class 47 No. 47624 *Cyclops* began life as D1763 and was first named after the mythical one-eyed creature at Bristol Bath Road Depot in 1966. Here it is at Sheffield in 1985. It spent the first twenty-five years of its career at Western Region depots, including Old Oak Common and Cardiff Canton. Withdrawal came for this Brush 4 in 2004, though it had been stored out of service as early as 1998.

No. 50037 Arrives at Paddington

Featuring Network SouthEast's distinctive multi-coloured livery, No. 50037 *Illustrious* pulls into Paddington station in September 1988. This version of the NSE livery rendered the cab windows white. An alternative version had blue windows. No. 50037 was withdrawn three years after this photograph in 1991.

Illustrious Arrival at Reading

A bright day at Reading in September 1988 sees Class 50 No. 50037 *Illustrious* standing at the platform with an Exeter to London Paddington service. It was rare for an entire rake of coaching stock to feature the Network SouthEast livery and this train is no exception, with at least one vehicle holding out in BR blue.

Ramillies arrives at Reading

On a rather murky 6 December 1982, rail blue-liveried Class 50 No. 50019 *Ramillies* pulls into Reading with a westbound service. At this time, there were only six Class 50s still carrying this livery, the rest having been outshopped in 'large logo' livery at Doncaster. (V. Hellam)

Freshly Refurbished 50 at Doncaster

Class 50 No. 50040 *Leviathan* (later *Centurion*) has just been turned out in superb condition following refurbishment at Doncaster Works in July 1985. Here it stands on the works release siding adjacent to the station. It was first re-liveried from overall BR blue at Doncaster in 1981. (V. Hellam)

Rare Mileage for No. 40012 on 'The Don and Fiddler'

This was a very rare appearance of a Class 40 on the Barnsley to Penistone branch. On 20 October 1984, No. 40012 is seen working hard as it lifts its train of Mk 1 stock up the gradient and past the site of Summer Lane station en route to Huddersfield. Even with a Class 47 banking, it's no walkover for the veteran Type 4, with the train loaded to twelve vehicles.

Blue and Green Motive Power at Burton Salmon

Another railtour that ran in the autumn of 1984, the 'Tees-Tyne Boggard', took a pair of Class 40s from Toton to Hartlepool and then to London King's Cross. Here Nos 40181 and 40122 power through Burton Salmon on the approach to York on the afternoon of 27 October.

The End of an Era Draws Near

A view taken inside Swindon Works in 1983, as former Longsight-based Class 40 No. 40159 awaits dismantling. Both the locomotive and the famous works would soon be confined to history.

Not Quite the End of the Road

Class 40 No. 40140 is seen here in a partially dismantled state at Derby Works in September 1982, following its withdrawal from Wigan's Springs Branch Depot. Despite appearances, it was later moved to Crewe, where it was cut up at the works there in the following year.

The Glorious Settle & Carlisle

It is the summer of 1984 and the Class 40s are entering the twilight of their careers. The S&C route still held out the prospect of seeing these classic machines in action however and on this August day the Carlisle to Leeds service featured No. 40099, seen here approaching Dent in the hazy afternoon sunshine.

Powering North on the S&C

Class 40 No. 40099 takes on the 'long drag' in style on 23 August 1984. The veteran machine is seen here storming through Dent with a Leeds to Carlisle service. The signal box was out of use by this date and was demolished shortly afterwards.

Almost Monochrome

The industrial environment of Manchester's Victoria station forms a virtually colour-free backdrop as Class 40 No. 40160 takes a rake of coke hoppers towards Miles Platting in April 1983. The station has been rationalised and visually transformed since those rather grimy but infinitely more atmospheric days.

Celebrating Twenty-Five Years of the 40s

The 'Silver Jubilee' railtour was organised in March 1983 to celebrate the quarter-century of the Class 40s in service. Here the tour departs Leeds behind Nos 40084 and 40086, destination London Euston.

Another Trans-Pennine Turn

The Type 4 Peaks gave many years' service on the trans-Pennine route via Standedge to Manchester and Liverpool. Here, No. 45113 pulls into Huddersfield station on one such turn in May 1982.

Victorian Grandeur of York

The unmistakeable sweeping roof of York station towers above Peak No. 45144 as it pulls in with a southbound passenger service in May 1986. Many Peaks had already been withdrawn by this stage. No. 45144 would last until December of the following year.

Fading Splendour of the Midland

The remains of Cudworth's main station building can be seen in the distance as Peak No. 45052 powers past the substantial stone-built signalbox with a passenger service in August 1979. The tall semaphore signals here still had a few years' life ahead of them but the end was in sight.

Unexpected Motive Power at Hellifield

A northbound West Coast express comes off the Blackburn line at Hellifield on 2 May 1987 during Bank Holiday engineering diversions. Somewhat unusually, the motive power on this occasion is provided not by the usual Class 47 but by No. 45124. This Peak was withdrawn later that year after catching fire at Leicester. (V. Hellam)

Full Order Book at Crewe

There are plenty of Class 47s to keep the repair shops busy at Crewe in this March 1984 view. Fronting a line of three Brush 4s is No. 47166, which began life as D1761 and assumed no fewer than three identities under the TOPS numbering system. After No. 47166 came No. 47611 and then No. 47837. Despite the investment being made in this picture, it was withdrawn by 1992.

Brush 4 in the Frame

A misty Horbury Station Junction is the location for this September 1984 shot of Class 47 No. 47347, which is approaching Healey Mills Yard with a short engineers' working. Previously D1828, this Loughborough-built machine was converted to Class 57 in 1999 and is still in service as No. 57004.

Powering North at Auchterarder

Class 47 No. 47470 *University of Edinburgh* puts down the power as it storms through Auchterarder with a Euston to Inverness service in August 1989. This locomotive was fitted with a replacement cab following serious crash damage in 1984. (V. Hellam)

Brush 4s in Action at Gleneagles

This July 1988 image shows Class 47-hauled services passing at Gleneagles. Approaching the well-kept station is No. 47479 while No. 47578 *The Royal Society of Edinburgh* waits at the platform. Both locomotives were subsequently repainted into Parcels Sector red livery in the 1990s. (V. Hellam)

Speed and Power Combine at Copmanthorpe

What better way to travel between Newcastle and Liverpool? Class 40 No. 40013, formerly *Andania*, storms past Copmanthorpe, south of York, with a trans-Pennine express in August 1984. Despite its healthy performance here, No. 40013 was withdrawn just five months later after failing an examination at Crewe, though it was subsequently preserved.

A Glorious Summer Saturday

This is how many enthusiasts will remember the Class 40s. On a superb August afternoon in 1983, No. 40085 arrives at Sheffield with the 13.20 Skegness to Manchester Piccadilly service. The revenue from haulage fans on these services was presumably substantial, as they often seemed to outnumber the 'ordinary' traveller. This particular locomotive was scrapped at Doncaster Works in 1984.

Routine Duty for No. 40002

A daily sight at Manchester Victoria – Class 40 No. 40002 trundles through the station with a rake of open wagons in April 1983, passing a Class 25 that is taking a break between banking duties.

Bound for the Refinery

Probably bound for the Stanlow oil refinery, a train of bulk tanks descends Miles Platting bank on the approach to Manchester Victoria in April 1983. Class 40 No. 40024, formerly *Lucania*, is the recipient of some detailed visual enhancement, including the application of a '9A' shed sticker, the steam-era code for Longsight.

On the Oil Tanks for Ecclesfield

Class 40 No. 40013, formerly *Andania*, waits for the right-away at Sheffield in July 1982 with a train of bulk oil tanks bound for the terminal at Ecclesfield, on the Barnsley line.

Kings of the Castle

The crew of Class 40 No. 40084 exchange some banter while their nicely turned-out machine is readied for the next leg of the journey from Cleethorpes to Red Bank with the newspapers. The photograph was taken at Sheffield on 24 July 1982.

Whistling Through Guide Bridge

A train of Presflo cement tanks heads through Guide Bridge station bound for the Hope Valley in October 1981. Class 40 No. 40013 provides the motive power on this occasion.

No. 40104 under the Gantries

Redundant electrification gantries frame Class 40 No. 40104 at Guide Bridge as it brings an eastbound cement train round the curve from Crowthorn Junction on the Ashton line in April 1983. This short stretch of freight-only line was lifted a few years later.

Up on the Jacks at Derby

Peak No. 45104 *The Royal Warwickshire Fusiliers* receives attention at Derby Works in March 1985. This particular Peak would remain in service for a further three years, being withdrawn in 1988 and scrapped in Glasgow in 1992.

How a Class 45 Should Look

Peak Class 45 No. 45144 *Royal Signals* is seen here in superb condition following an overhaul at Crewe in March 1984. The beautifully turned-out locomotive was sadly to enjoy a mere three more years in service. It was cut up at Vic Berry's yard in Leicester in the summer of 1988.

The Long and Short of It

A compact ICI-liveried shunter awaits its next turn as Class 45 No. 45075, just a few inches short of 69 feet in length, arrives at Great Rocks Junction on a light engine move from Buxton in April 1983. The Peak will reverse here and work down to nearby Tunstead to pick up a loaded aggregates train. (V. Hellam)

Heavy Duty Ballast on the Old Road

The former Great Central route from Chesterfield to Rotherham, avoiding Sheffield, is known as the 'Old Road' and here in July 1982 Peak No. 46014 heads north at Treeton with a well-loaded ballast train. The semaphores in this picture were controlled by Treeton South Junction signal box, which closed not long after.

Tidy Looking Type 4 at Crewe Electric Depot

The application of 'sector'-based liveries to the Class 47 fleet in the 1990s gave a much needed smartening up to these long-serving machines. Here No. 47053 *Dollands Moor International* looks in fine condition as it stands at Crewe Electric Depot during the Open Day of October 1994. Sadly it was scrapped in 2007.

New Sector Identification for No. 47033

Tinsley-based Class 47 No. 47033 *The Royal Logistic Corps* looks superb in its new Railfreight Distribution livery at Crewe Electric Depot. The locomotive was on display on the occasion of the May 1997 Open Day. Somewhat remarkably, this Crewe-built machine would be classified as 'stored unserviceable' as little as two years later. It was cut up in 2008.

Sulzer Profiles at Waverley

Resting between turns at Edinburgh's principal station, Class 47 No. 47712 *Lady Diana Spencer* and BRCW Type 2 No. 27017 present contrasting profiles when seen in June 1985. The pale blue stripe on the Brush Type 4 was a distinctive ScotRail touch. This Class 47 is still operational today and carries the same livery, though in the intermediate years it carried a variety of other colours and names.

Daybreak at Inverness

Steam condenses in the cool air as two Class 47s prepare to depart Inverness with early morning services in June 1985. On the left is No. 47210, while snowplough-fitted No. 47546 *Aviemore Centre* is on the adjacent platform. At this time the Brush 4s were still sharing the Scottish Highland routes with their Sulzer-engined Class 27 cousins.

Class 50s in Cornish Finale

Celebrating the end of Class 50s in main line service, the 'Cornish Caper' tour ran from York to Penzance over the weekend of 18 and 19 March 1994, including a trip on the Newquay branch. Motive power was provided by Nos 50007, 50033 and 50050, the latter seen here at Plymouth on the outward leg.

Nos 50007 and 50050 at Plymouth

A rain-swept Plymouth station hosts Class 50s Nos 50007 and 50050 as they wait with the outward leg of the 'Cornish Caper' railtour of March 1994. Starting in York with Class 47 haulage on the Friday evening, the tour reached Penzance at about 10.00 on Saturday morning.

Waiting for the Next Turn at New Street

A light engine movement for Class 50 No. 50036 *Victorious* as it prepares for its next passenger turn at Birmingham New Street in April 1987. At this time it was possible to see diesel, electric and HST-operated services here in addition to many EMU and DMU diagrams.

Unusual Duo at Sheffield

A pair of large logo Class 50s make a rather unusual sight as they tick over on one of the through roads at Sheffield station on the morning of 12 October 1984. Nos 50017 *Royal Oak* and 50038 *Formidable* were probably en route to Doncaster for attention at the Plant. (V. Hellam)

The Centre of Attention

The date is August 1984 and all eyes are on No. 40012 *Aureol* as it blasts away from its Sheffield stop with a Skegness to Manchester Piccadilly service on a bright Saturday afternoon. The facility to spend an entire journey leaning out of a window is still available in 2018 courtesy of the surviving HST fleet, though the demand is not what it was.

'The Dore-Mat' Passes Barnsley

A February afternoon in 1984 sees Class 40 No. 40024, formerly *Lucania*, passing Jumble Lane level crossing at Barnsley with this railtour, which took haulage fans from Birmingham to Matlock via Crewe, Huddersfield, Tinsley and Doncaster, covering some freight-only routes and featuring five different locomotives.

Heavily Loaded Minerals Head for the Pennines

Class 40 No. 40022, once named *Laconia*, approaches Huddersfield with a well-loaded westbound mineral working on 2 October 1981. A Lancashire power station is the probable destination.

Atmospheric Kirkgate

Wakefield Kirkgate's Platform 1 is shrouded in exhaust fumes courtesy of No. 40070. Having been held at a signal, the locomotive is accelerating away from a standing start with predictable results. The picture dates from July 1980.

No. 40035 Takes the Tanks Through Sheffield

Left on its own after the removal of a Class 25 earlier, No. 40035, formerly *Apapa*, takes the BOC tanks through Sheffield en route to Ditton in August 1983. A Class 40/25 or pair of Class 40s was the usual motive power for this train at the time.

Diesels Under the Woodhead Gantries

On the once-electrified stretch between Tinsley Yard and Woodburn Junction in Sheffield, Class 40 No. 40131 is partnered with Type 2 No. 25313 on the Broughton Lane to Ditton empty BOC tanks in July 1983, two years after the wires came down.

Summer Passenger Duty

This is Chester station in July 1979, and Class 40 No. 40166 pulls in with a North Wales service comprised of Mk 1 coaching stock. The loco has yet to be fitted with the standard 'domino' headcode panel insert and is instead displaying the default four zeros that were adopted when train reporting numbers were deemed superfluous in the late '70s.

Ex-Works Machine at Chester

Class 40 No. 40115 is fresh from an overhaul at Crewe – the last of its working life – and looks very smart in this image from Chester station in July 1979. The Longsight-based machine was working a North Wales passenger turn on this occasion. It lasted another three years in traffic.

Double Vision at Sheffield

A June 1983 shot of two Class 45s standing at the north end of Sheffield station – then very much a routine event, but not for long. On the left, No. 45114 has arrived on a passenger service while recently ex-works No. 45134 is on a light engine move, possibly to nearby Nunnery Sidings.

Named Peaks at Sheffield

In the summer of 1982 it was still possible to see Peak-hauled trains on the St Pancras and North East–South West routes, and sights like this one at Sheffield were relatively common, though none the less welcome for all that. Nos 45137 *Bedfordshire & Hertfordshire Regiment (T.A.)* and 45111 *Grenadier Guardsman* are seen at the north end of the station on 19 June.

A Peak at Speed

A beautiful spring afternoon at Church Fenton sees Peak No. 45150 powering through on a southbound express in April 1984. The station here has seen much rationalisation since then, with the original buildings and signal box long gone.

Northbound at Colton

A northbound express storms through Colton South Junction near York in April 1984. Peak Class 45 No. 45114 has a rake of mainly air-conditioned Mk 2 stock in tow. Today this service will probably be formed of a rather shorter Class 220 unit.

One of Many Previous Identities

Class 47 No. 47817 began life as Crewe-built D1611, later becoming No. 47032 and then No. 47662. It was renumbered as No. 47817 in 1989 and carried several liveries in that guise, including the distinctive Porterbrook shade seen here at Tinsley's Open Day in 1996. This is one of the fleet subsequently re-built as a Class 57 in 2003.

Echoes of the LNWR

In Waterman Railways' lined black livery, Class 47 No. 47705 *Guy Fawkes* stands on display at the Crewe Basford Hall Open Day event in August 1995 prior to its naming ceremony by owner Pete Waterman. Later rebuilt as Class 57 No. 57303, this locomotive carried a bewildering array of liveries in its lifetime as a Type 4, including BR blue, NSE, ScotRail and RES colours.

Dedicated to Freight Haulage

One of the Class 47/3 sub-class that was built specifically for freight haulage and therefore never fitted with train heating equipment, No. 47310 passes the old Manchester Exchange platforms with a bulk oil turn in August 1984. This was an Eastern Region machine throughout its life, being allocated to several depots including Tinsley, Healey Mills, Thornaby, Knottingley, Immingham and Stratford.

Type 4 Banking Power

A view looking west from Summer Lane station in Barnsley as the 'Don & Fiddler' railtour of October 1984 disappears towards Penistone. Tinsley's Class 47 No. 47316 applies the power to assist train engine No. 40012 *Aureol* with the lengthy consist.

Dauntless at Clapham Junction

Class 50 No. 50048 *Dauntless* is seen at Clapham Junction during a light engine move in September 1988. The class enjoyed a new lease of life in the Network SouthEast era, though this example, like many others, was withdrawn by the summer of 1991.

Exeter Approaching Clapham Junction

With the usual complement of nine coaches, a Paddington to Exeter service approaches Clapham Junction in September 1988 with the appropriately named No. 50044 in charge. Withdrawn three years later, No. 50044 was subsequently preserved.

A Sylvan Setting on the Berks & Hants Route

Class 50 No. 50045 *Achilles* winds through the glorious countryside of the Berks & Hants route near Bedwyn with a London-bound service in July 1987. At this stage No. 50045 had only three years' service left ahead of it, though it was not cut up until 2000.

Uniform Colour Scheme on NSE

On this occasion a Network SouthEast-liveried locomotive was paired with a matching rake of coaches, as Class 50 No. 50035 *Ark Royal* heads an Oxford to Paddington service through leafy Ruscombe in June 1988. This particular Type 4 machine had only two years of main line service ahead of it, after which it would become the first of the class to be preserved. (V. Hellam)

Skegness Substitute at Sheffield

With evidence of recent railtour duty in the form of white buffers and red buffer beam, Class 40 No. 40077 stands at Sheffield with a Skegness–Manchester Piccadilly service, which it had taken over from a failed No. 40080 earlier. The date was 18 September 1982.

Seating Not Required for Haulage Fans

Presumably some enthusiasts would be seated, but many chose to stand at the windows of the numerous summer Saturday trains that ran between the cities and seaside towns in the 1980s. Here a Skegness-bound service arrives at Sheffield behind No. 40013, formerly *Andania*, in August 1983.

Crewe-Bound Cavalcade

Class 40 No. 40118 pauses on one of Huddersfield's through roads with a trio of locomotives en route from York to Crewe Works in November 1981. The two Class 47s and single Class 25 will travel via Stalybridge and Stockport to reach their destination. No. 40118 is currently in preservation at Tyseley.

Empty Stock Arrival at Leeds

The deserted platforms of Leeds station form the backdrop to this image of Class 40 No. 40020, formerly *Franconia*, arriving with a train of empty Mk 1 stock in May 1982. No. 40020 was very close to the end of its working life at this stage. It was withdrawn just three months later.

Summer Evening Type 4s

Sheffield could be relied upon to provide a steady stream of Type 4 action in the early 1980s, and this July evening in 1982 was no exception. One of many Peak-hauled passenger services prepares to depart in the background, while on Platform 1 Healey Mills-based No. 40006 waits with a bulk oil turn.

Classic Traction for the Harwich Boat Train

Manchester Piccadilly in May 1982, and Class 40 No. 40015, formerly *Aquitania*, waits to take the Harwich service over the Pennines to Sheffield, as many of these locomotives will have done over the years.

D200 Arrives at Snowy Huddersfield

The 'St Andrew' railtour of 9 February 1985 was hauled by celebrity Class 40 D200 from Bolton to Edinburgh and back. Here it is greeted by a gaggle of photographers at Huddersfield on the outward journey. A train heating failure meant a two-hour hiatus at Newcastle, after which the tour never recovered its original timings.

The North Briton Tour at Stonehaven

One of many tours to advertise Class 40 motive power in the 1980s, this one featured No. 40086, seen here on a photo stop at Stonehaven. This was on the outward leg of a tour that took passengers from Huddersfield to Aberdeen in March 1984. The event was organised by the Class 40 Preservation Society.

In the Days of Carriage Sidings

Nunnery Carriage Sidings provided much-needed capacity for locomotive-hauled stock at Sheffield in the pre-Sprinter era. Here, Peak No. 45134 stands at the head of a rake of Mk 1 stock in July 1982. A redundant gantry from the Woodhead electrification can be seen to the left.

Through the Heartland of Yorkshire Industry

The Midland main line at Wath ran through the centre of the giant Manvers coking plant, which can be seen in the background of this shot. Peak No. 45036 sweeps through Wath Road Junction with a Sheffield-bound passenger service in the summer of 1980.

Contrasting Diesel Profiles at Sheffield

One of Sheffield's lamp standards harks back to the days when it was necessary to distinguish between this station and its Great Central neighbour. Class 46 No. 46026, in tidy external condition, waits to go north while an HST unit stands on a St Pancras service in the foreground in this 1983 image.

Type 4 Tonnage at Basford Hall

The two Class 47s are the relative lightweights in this impressive line-up at Crewe's Basford Hall Open Day in 1995. Bookending the quartet are Class 40 No. 40135 and Class 45 D120, the latter carrying its original number. In the TOPS era this was No. 45108.

Northbound Railfreight Service at Masborough

Rotherham Masborough's Platforms 3 and 4 look well maintained and tidy in this July 1982 image, even though neither had regular passenger use at this time. Class 47 No. 47145 heads off the Chesterfield line with a northbound freight. No. 47145 later carried Fragonset blue livery and was named *Myrddin Emrys*. It survived until 2008 and was cut up at Stockton.

Backdrop of Wild Boar Fell

A Carlisle to Leeds service approaches the summit of the Settle & Carlisle line at Ais Gill on 17 June 1989. Large logo-liveried Class 47 No. 47597 provides the motive power for this service, which has been strengthened to ten coaches on this occasion. This Type 4 had earlier carried the number 47026. It was later renumbered to No. 47741 and named *Resilient*.

Storming Away From New Street

Shortly before the end of locomotive-hauled services on the cross-country routes, Class 47 No. 47812 powers away from Birmingham New Street on a southbound service in September 2002. No. 47812 carried three previous identities – Nos D1916, 47239 and 47657. It is still in service today.

Waiting With the Mail at Crewe

A very common scene at Crewe during the 1980s – overnight mail waits to go north with Class 47 No. 47349 in charge on 11 April 1985. One of the batch built with no train heating capability, this Brush 4 was later rebuilt and is enjoying a new lease of life as Type 5 No. 57603 *Tintagel Castle*.

All That Remained of Cudworth

A humble brick building serving as a stores shed for the PW crew is all that remained of the Midland's once extensive station at Cudworth, near Barnsley, by the time of this picture in August 1979. Class 47 No. 47406 puts out a burst of exhaust as it accelerates through on a southbound passenger service.

Rural South Yorkshire Scene

This is the Barnsley to Penistone branch, looking from Dodworth towards Silkstone in the summer of 1980. Class 47 No. 47304 tows Type 5 No. 56001 to Wath Depot for servicing. A freight-only section of line at the time, this route was later used for the Sheffield–Huddersfield service when the former GC route via Deepcar was truncated in the wake of the Woodhead closure.

Returning on the Bishop's Triple

This railtour of 5 June 1993 had taken a triple-header of Class 50s to York, with a pair then returning to Bishop's Lydeard. Here, D400 (No. 50050) and No. 50033 *Glorious* have climbed the chord from Mexborough to Swinton in South Yorkshire and are heading towards Sheffield on the former Midland main line.

Class 50s on North Yorkshire Tour Duty

An ambitious itinerary saw this Pathfinder Tours trip of November 1992 run from Eastleigh to York and return, with Nos 50007 and 50033 working from Bristol Temple Meads and back. Here the pair passes Pannal on the Leeds to Harrogate route with green-liveried No. 50007 *Sir Edward Elgar* leading.

Star Attraction at Sheffield

Class 50s returning to the Western Region after attention at Doncaster Works would often make an appearance on cross-country passenger services, but occasionally an example would work north and south on one day. Here, in the summer of 1983, No. 50003 *Temeraire* attracts a crowd at Sheffield as it departs for Plymouth after earlier working through from the South West to York.

Refurbishment Overdue for No. 50024

Class 50 No. 50024 *Vanguard* is seen passing Sheffield en route to Doncaster Works for refurbishment in June 1982. The locomotive still sports the original cab front appearance, with no high-intensity headlight, and looks to be in rather poor cosmetic condition. No. 50024 had just less than a decade of service left ahead of it at the time of this picture, being scrapped at Old Oak Common in 1991.

A Reddish Summer Evening

There were plenty of Class 40s to be found stabled at Reddish Depot near Manchester in the summer of 1982. Here on a July evening, split-headcode No. 40141 basks in the sunshine outside the shed. Class 25 No. 25326 is behind. The overhead wires were still used by Class 506 multiple units.

Mixed Bag for No. 40004

A bright August afternoon in 1984 sees Class 40 No. 40004 drift down the bank at Miles Platting with a short rake of miscellaneous wagons. Any attempt to display an accurate headcode arrangement has clearly been abandoned, as this is far from being a regal working.

Classic Territory

Crewe enjoyed a long association with the Class 40s and they were a daily sight at the depot, station and nearby locomotive works up to the mid-1980s. Here, in May 1980, No. 40112 waits with a service for North Wales while No. 40023, formerly *Lancastria*, pulls away in the foreground.

Lowly Duty for No. 40004

The summer of 1983 saw many Class 40s employed on the seasonal holiday services, but for some it was very much business as usual with a range of humble freight and engineering duties. Here, No. 40004 stands at Crewe during modernisation works at the south end of the station. Withdrawal for this machine came the following year and it was cut up here at the nearby Crewe Works.

Fertiliser Failure at Hellifield

Class 40 No. 40099 comes to the rescue of failed classmate No. 40145 at Hellifield. The pair is seen at the head of a UKF fertiliser working in April 1980. (V. Hellam)

On the Ballast Through Horbury

A dull December day in 1982 sees Class 40 No. 40074 heading away from Horbury Junction in the direction of Healey Mills yard with a loaded ballast working. The Class 40s were once synonymous with this location.

Lightweight Freight Duty for Heavyweight Machine

A train of empty mineral wagons is unlikely to be proving much of a test for Class 40 No. 40183. Here, the EE heavyweight negotiates Crowthorn Junction on the Ashton Moss line and enters Guide Bridge station with this eastbound working in May 1982.

Into the Winter Sun at Dringhouses

An overtaking East Coast express affords the opportunity to capture a view of Class 40 No. 40183 heading south with a mixed freight past Dringhouses Yard, near York, in November 1981.

Sunlit Memories of the Midland Main Line

The evening sun illuminates Peak No. 45143 in this evocative image from Sheffield in August 1983. The nameplate *5th Royal Inniskilling Dragoon Guards* provides a distinctive focal point. Unlike the Class 40s, the Peaks thankfully retained their proud military names during the 'corporate' BR era.

Peak Super Power at Sheffield

It was almost unheard of for Peaks to work in pairs under normal circumstances, so we must assume that train engine No. 45012 had suffered some kind of problem that required assistance for this northbound service at Sheffield. Class 46 No. 46046 is seen here providing the necessary traction in June 1982.

Last of the Split-Headcode Peaks

Peak No. 45053 survived with its original split-headcode configuration up to its withdrawal from traffic in late 1983, being scrapped at Crewe before it could be converted to the sealed beam headlight arrangement that had by then become standard on the class. It is seen here at Crewe Works in March 1984.

Demise of the Type 4s

A rather sombre image from Derby Works in March 1985 as the era of Type 4 dominance approaches its zenith. In the centre, Peak No. 45045, formerly *Coldstream Guardsman*, is partially dismantled and will soon be cut up at Vic Berry's scrapyard in Leicester; on the right, Class 40 No. 40132 awaits the same fate.

All Consigned to History

The southern end of Tinsley Depot plays host to numerous withdrawn and active locomotives in this 1993 view. Nearest to the flower-strewn embankment are Class 47s Nos 47222 and 47060. There is no railway infrastructure at this location any more, and all traces of the depot have now disappeared beneath commercial development. No. 47060, however, does survive in Class 57 guise as No. 57008.

Sunny Afternoon by the Seaside

If only days like this could be re-created… Class 47 No. 47211 waits to depart Scarborough in what was then very much an everyday event in August 1982. Alongside is another Type 4 in the shape of Class 40 No. 40029, formerly *Saxonia*, while the little yard on the right contains, among other things, Class 31 No. 31219.

Sulzer Machines Meet at Victoria

In the rather grimy environs of Manchester Victoria station, Class 47 No. 47340 passes another Sulzer-engined machine in the form of Class 25 No. 25323, which is acting as banker for freights that require a helping hand on nearby Miles Platting bank. No. 47340 later appeared in Railfreight 'red stripe' livery and then in 'Dutch' engineer's grey and yellow colours.

Contrasting Class 47s at Reading

The late 1980s saw the Class 47 fleet carrying a range of liveries, including these two seen at Reading in September 1988. While NSE-liveried No. 47583 *County of Hertfordshire* waits on a passenger service at the platform, No. 47019, in large logo Railfreight grey, storms through with a container service. Neither locomotive survives today.

Rain-Lashed 50 at Crewe

Crewe station in the early hours of 4 September 1984 and Class 50 No. 50003 *Temeraire* waits to go south with a parcels service. A large number of mail services were loaded during the hours of darkness at Crewe in the 1980s, providing a wide range of motive power of both diesel and electric varieties.

Smoky Line-Up at Plymouth

Plymouth station in March 1994, and the three Class 50s that have provided the motive power for Pathfinder Tours'‘Cornish Caper’ stand side by side during a photo stop – from left to right, Nos 50007, 50033 and 50050. For good measure an HST units adds to the atmospheric mix.

Capital Stabling Point for No. 50033

Class 50 No. 50033 *Glorious* is seen here sharing a bay platform at London's Waterloo terminus with a Class 73 electro-diesel in the days when locomotive-hauled trains could still be seen in the capital. The Class 50s saw regular service on the Exeter St Davids service at this time.

St Vincent at Paddington

London's Paddington terminus had a lengthy association with the Class 50s after they had been cascaded onto Western Region express work following their deployment on the pre-electrified West Coast Main Line. Here, No. 50004 *St Vincent* moves away from the buffers after working in from Devon in September 1988.

Unforgettable Summer Saturdays at the Seaside

Summer holiday trains were guaranteed to bring a multiplicity of loco-hauled trains to the seaside termini of Britain. Here at Scarborough we see an evocative scene with Class 40 No. 40029 *Saxonia* waiting with empty stock for an evening working to Wakefield in August 1982.

En Route to the East Lancs Railway

Two resplendent preserved Class 40s trundle through Derby on their way to the East Lancashire Railway at Bury in February 2017. Leading is No. 345, formerly No. 40145, with split-headcode No. 40135, fresh from a repaint, behind. The latter is yet to have its number and 'double arrow' symbol applied.

Frontal Modification for No. 40133

A permanent solution to the issue of draughty nose-end doors was to weld up the front of the locomotive, as seen here in the case of No. 40133. The other end of the loco, however, retained the original configuration. It is seen here passing the site of Manchester Exchange station in April 1983.

Surplus to Requirements

A tell-tale heap of sand at the side of the track gives away the fact that this Class 40 will work no more trains. Tractive assistance will not be necessary now that No. 40136 has been withdrawn from traffic and here it stands with similarly doomed Class 76s at Reddish in July 1982.

Awaiting the Right-Away at Victoria

Once an everyday scene at Manchester's Victoria station, No. 40194 waits to depart with a trans-Pennine service on a damp day in August 1982. The coaching stock looks to be predominantly of Mk 1 vintage.

Heading the Vans to Nunnery Sidings

As Class 45 No. 45116 stands at the platform with a northbound passenger turn, No. 40027, formerly *Parthia*, waits for its crew change at a damp Sheffield station in June 1982 before heading to Nunnery Sidings with a train of newspaper vans.

Double-Heading the BOC Tanks at Broughton Lane

Once one of Sheffield's district stations, Broughton Lane was long-closed by the time of this picture in July 1983, though the nearby goods yard and BOC depot were still *in situ*. Here Class 40 No. 40022, formerly *Laconia*, and Class 25 No. 25230 head past the remnants of one of the station platforms.

Guide Bridge Shunt for No. 40168

Longsight-based No. 40168 propels a train of mineral hoppers into the yard at Dewsnap to the east of Guide Bridge station in September 1982. This picture shows the complex track layout here to good effect.

Peak in the Frame at Masborough

Rotherham's Masborough station was ideally situated to catch both freight and passenger traffic on the former Midland and Great Central routes to the north of Sheffield. Here Class 46 No. 46037, with central headcode panel still *in situ*, waits for a path with a train of bolster wagons in October 1983.

Classic Rolling Stock at New Mills

Who knows how many trips to and from the quarries of the Buxton area these classic ICI aggregates hoppers will have made over the years? Dating from the steam era, and once no doubt hauled by Class 9F locomotives, they are seen here at New Mills behind Peak No. 45076 in August 1984.

Coasting Downgrade from Barnsley

A seven-coach summer Saturday service from Weymouth coasts down the grade from Barnsley towards Darton with Peak No. 45007 in charge. Bound for Bradford, the train will take the Healey Mills route at Crigglestone Junction, a line not used by regular passenger services. The date is July 1981.

Ballast Duty for No. 45050

A train of loaded ballast hoppers makes its way past the site of Horbury & Ossett station and towards Healey Mills yard behind Peak No. 45050 in July 1983. A classic West Yorkshire mill stands behind. Photographs taken in this vicinity today reveal a proliferation of vegetation growth, much of it the invasive buddleia. (V. Hellam)

Bulk Oil Going North at Colton

Class 47 No. 47151 heads north on the four-track section of former Midland main line at Colton South Junction near York in April 1984. Its train of bulk oil tanks is almost certainly destined for Teesside. The railway landscape here remains virtually unchanged in 2018 as successive governments prevaricate over electrification of this route.

Decline and Fall

A train of empty sand hoppers from the Monk Bretton glassworks at Barnsley waits on the former Midland main line at Cudworth North Junction in October 1984. Brush Type 4 No. 47338 stands among the many forlorn remnants of an earlier era, soon to be completely swept away. The line to Monk Bretton, however, survives at the time of writing. (V. Hellam)

Distinctive Livery for No. 47614

A superb July afternoon at Sheffield in 1985 sees large logo Class 47 No. 47614 standing on one of the station's centre roads. This locomotive, then numbered D1733, had the distinction of being chosen to carry the experimental XP64 blue livery in 1964 which was the precursor to the long-lived Monastral Blue that subsequently became standard throughout the BR fleet.

Steel Coil Empties on the Midland Main Line

Colas Rail's Class 47 No. 47749 *City of Truro* approaches Attenborough on the Trent Junction to Nottingham route in April 2017. The veteran machine is working the Washwood Heath to Boston Docks empty steel coil service. This particular Brush 4 has carried no fewer than three other names, most recently *Demelza* from 2007, but it reverted to its original in 2016.

Greeting the New Year at Hellifield

An image dating from 3 January 1986, and bright winter sunshine illuminates Class 47 No. 47479 as it accelerates onto the Skipton line at Hellifield with a Carlisle to Leeds service. Passengers on the vintage Mk 1 stock will have been treated to the sight of snow-capped peaks as the train traversed the S&C on this day.

A Machine of Many Identities

Another of the Class 47s that has carried multiple identities, No. 47854 *Women's Royal Voluntary Service* sweeps through Blea Moor in April 2004 with a diverted West Coast express. This Type 4 was built as D1972 and then carried the numbers 47271, 47604 and 47674 before assuming its current identity in 1995. It remains in service as part of the WCRC fleet.

Tinsley Type 4 Trio

Tinsley Depot hosted an open day on 27 April 1996, its last before closure. Here a trio of preserved Class 50s is seen on display at the south end of the shed. From left to right are Nos 50044 *Exeter*, 50033 *Glorious* and 50007 *Sir Edward Elgar*.

Departmental Circular

Class 50 No. 50008 *Thunderer* was deployed on a Network Rail circular inspection tour from Derby Technical Centre in August 2017. Here it is seen approaching Attenborough on the outward leg. The itinerary took in Lincoln, Chesterfield and Worksop, territory once very unfamiliar to this class.

Parcels Duty for No. 40034

Another mundane yet essential diagram for a veteran Type 4, as No. 40034, formerly *Accra*, brings a train of newspaper vans into Manchester Victoria in April 1983. The train is passing the former Exchange platforms, the site of a car park now that the number of lines here has been drastically reduced.

Distinctive Appearance

Reddish Depot in February 1983, and among just three Class 40s on shed that day was Longsight-allocated No. 40093, looking very distinctive with red buffer beam and silver draw gear and buffers. At this stage No. 40093 had less than a year left in traffic.

Far From the Madding Crowd

Class 40 No. 40068 found itself on a very quiet backwater in November 1982 when it was called upon to assist in the dismantling of the former Dearne Valley Railway line between Goldthorpe colliery and Barnburgh. It is seen here near the headshunt limit on the outskirts of the pit.

A Change is as Good as a Rest for No. 40097

Class 40 No. 40097 takes a break at Sheffield station after working in with the BOC tanks to Broughton Lane with partner No. 40155 in June 1982. It later worked a passenger service to Manchester Piccadilly.

Summer Lane Heat Haze

Peak No. 45006 *Honourable Artillery Company* passes the site of Barnsley's Summer Lane station on a light engine move in June 1981. The loco is working from Wath Depot to Dodworth colliery, from where it will take an MGR service to Barnsley Junction at Penistone, for onward transit via the Woodhead route to Fiddler's Ferry power station.

Winter Railtour Duty for No. 45110

Class 45 No. 45110 heads away from Claydon Junction and towards Bedford via Bletchley with the 'Red Brick Rambler' railtour of 15 November 1986. The unusual itinerary took this tour from London Marylebone to Stainforth & Hatfield in Yorkshire, then back to St Pancras. (V. Hellam)

Hazy May Day at Sheffield

This Class 45 would not retain its single centre headcode panel for much longer. No. 45147 is seen at Sheffield on a hazy afternoon in May 1982. The Class 45s appeared with no fewer than four front-end styles, if the final sealed beam marker light type is included.

A Quiet Resting Place for No. 45023

Peak No. 45023 *The Royal Pioneer Corps* stands quietly at the buffers at Scarborough station after arrival with a summer Saturday service in August 1982. This was very much a routine sight back then, but within a short time these locomotive-hauled seaside trains would be consigned to history.

Light Engine Manoeuvre at York

A shunting manoeuvre at York shed sees Class 46 No. 46006 propelled onto the station avoiding lines on 31 May 1982, the date of the Pope's famous visit to the city. Despite the fresh-looking front end, this particular Peak was already destined for the scrapyard. It had been withdrawn for some time by this stage, though it was not finally cut up until 1985.

Open to the Public

Peak Class 45 No. 45108 receives a thorough inspection from visitors to Derby Works Open Day in September 1982. It was one of many withdrawn locomotives on the premises that day, including representatives of Classes 25, 27 and 40. No. 45108 was subsequently saved for preservation. (V. Hellam)

Scarborough-Bound Peak at Lime Street

A rather grim October afternoon in 1984 sees Peak No. 45140 waiting to depart Liverpool's Lime Street terminus with a trans-Pennine service for Scarborough. It is a journey that this locomotive will have made on many previous occasions.

Shovels at the Ready

There are no power tools in evidence for this trio of track workers, seen at the northerly end of Sheffield station in August 1983. Rumbling into the soot-stained tunnels with a train of Mk 1 stock is Class 46 No. 46026 *Leicestershire & Derbyshire Yeomanry*, the only one of the Class 46s to be named at that time.

Cement on the Move at Stockport Junction

Bescot-based Class 47 No. 47074 rounds the curve from Stockport Junction and into Guide Bridge station with a train of cement tanks in April 1983. The signal box here has long since gone and a huge amount of vegetation growth has transformed the view. This locomotive later spent a short time as No. 47646 and also as No. 47852 before withdrawal in 1991.

Twelve Coaches over the 'Long Drag'

The Pendolino services that currently operate on the West Coast Main Line have at least maintained some parity with the train lengths of the locomotive-hauled era, unlike many services operated by multiple units on other routes. The norm in 1985 is represented by this diverted Glasgow service, powering through Dent on the S&C line in April 1985. Class 47 No. 47466 does the honours.

West Coast Railways Empty Stock Move at Colton

The maroon livery of the WCRC fleet has become familiar across the national network. Still going strong in 2017, No. 47760 speeds north at Colton Junction with empty stock from Carnforth to Scarborough, seen on 3 October. This steam heat-fitted Brush Type 4 was built at Loughborough in 1964 as D1617.

Generation Gap at York

The latest generation of diesel power in the form of Class 68 No. 68003 *Astute* stands alongside Brush Type 4 stalwart No. 47854 *Diamond Jubilee* at York in August 2016. The Class 47 has carried its current name since 2012. It could be argued that the Crewe-built machine still looks reasonably modern alongside its twenty-first-century companion, despite the fifty-year gap in design evolution.

Original Look for Brush Type 4

Superbly turned-out Class 47 D1645 (No. 47830) *Beeching Legacy* sweeps through Thornhill on the G&SW route with an empty stock move from Kilmarnock to Swindon. The date was 14 May 2016. (V. Hellam)

Type 4s Power On in the Twenty-First Century

Crossing the Clyde at Crawford, a pair of Class 50s takes the 'Caledonian' special north on 7 October 2017. No. 50007, also carrying the number D407, leads No. 50049 on this tour from Euston to Glasgow, which marked the fiftieth anniversary of the introduction to traffic of these English Electric Type 4s. (V. Hellam)

The six principal classes of diesel locomotive that once made up the 'Type 4' classification – the 40, 44, 45, 46, 47 and 50 – were the survivors of a wider group that can trace its origins to the British Transport Commission's Modernisation Plan of 1955. Designating a power output of between 2,000 and 3,000 hp, the type once contained representatives of several non-standard and one-off prototype builds, including the Warship and Western diesel-hydraulics, which between them originally numbered over 100 examples. The scrapping, exporting or accidental writing off of the numerous Type 4 prototypes in the 1960s and early 1970s – with the exception of the ten Class 44 Peaks – left a cohort of over 900 diesel-electrics that became the real backbone of the BR fleet, including the most numerous single mainline class ever built in Britain, the 'Brush 4' – or Class 47, as it later became.

This pictorial collection presents a wide-ranging selection of images of Type 4 locomotives from the late 1970s to the present day, photographed and compiled by Andrew Walker and John Walker with contributions from fellow photographer Vaughan Hellam.

AMBERLEY   £14.99
ISBN 978-1-4456-8009-5
9 781445 680095
www.amberley-books.com